MW01534807

My Heart to Yours

Words to Enlighten and Inspire

To Amanda –
Thank you for your
open, loving heart!
Love,
Darlene
9-14-12

Darlene Carter

My Heart to Yours

1st Edition © 2012 Darlene Carter

ISBN: 978-0-9839777-3-5

This book was printed in the United States of America

Journey of a Dream Press
P.O. Box 1565
Duluth, GA 30096

www.JourneyofaDream.com

Dedicated to my sister who shares her heart, courage, and unconditional love with everyone she meets.

Thank you for a lifetime of love and inspiration.

Table of Contents

I have many sisters of Spirit
But only one of blood, bone, and DNA.
Parental cells mix together, miraculously
Creating two unique individuals,
Linked forever in a common bond of love and family.

Not fully appreciated in childhood;
Sisterly love matures in adulthood,
Becoming a tether to sanity;
Unimaginable to be without.

When this sister of flesh is also a sister of Spirit,
It is a miracle unparalleled,
And we celebrate each other;
Loving and being loved as only sisters can.

I am from a South of long ago;
Innocence and prejudice,
Dirt roads and bare feet.

I am from bike rides and roller skating,
Hoola Hoops and Hop Scotch,
And all games played outside.

I am from movies shown in theatres or drive-ins,
TV with only three channels, no remote control or color,
Record players and two-sided 45's with one song on each.

I am from a time before CD's, DVD's, or Facebook.
One amazing computer took up a whole room,
Holding less data than a thumb drive I now carry in a pocket.

I am from warm summer nights
Lightning bugs and hide and seek.
The smell of rain on a red dirt road
And stars so close I could almost touch them.

I am from laughter and sorrow,
Mixed together in the exotic elixir of life;
I am from yesterday and today;
Anticipating the miracles of tomorrow.

Things I Love

I love . . . .
The laughter of babies
A toddler's courage and exploration
A crisp, clear morning in the Fall
The smiles of my grandchildren
Butterflies and hummingbirds
Walking in the rain
Warm, sweet mornings in the Spring
Stars at night - Seeing the moon in the daytime.

Flowers and dirt
The smell of grass freshly cut
A blue cloudless sky
A sky with clouds that stir my imagination
Koi, cats (even though they make me sneeze)
And caterpillars
A beautiful song or a silly song
Adult children who make me proud
Chocolate *sigh*
Time alone with me

Writing and reading and watching TV
Movies that make me cry
Movies that make me laugh
Computer and email
Swinging and rocking - alone or with someone
Watching the ocean do what it does
Sitting on the sand - playing or not
Snow and hot chocolate
Breathing for an hour and feeling time stand still!

Things I Love . . . About Me!

I love my . . . .
Body
Courage
Honesty
Compassion
Sense of humor
Creativity
Dedication to my family

I love that I can. . . .
Listen to a friend's pain and not own it
Spend time with myself and enjoy my own company
Honor my commitments and not feel resentment
Shed tears of joy or sorrow and know the difference
Listen to the sounds of the earth and be comforted
Tell the truth gently
Laugh abundantly
Play in the rain.

I love being a . . . .
Wife
Mother
Grandmother
Friend
Writer
Breather
Person with integrity.

Each day I celebrate all that I am and will be!

I'm not twelve anymore
And that just sucks!

Mostly it's my body that doesn't want
to play like a preteen anymore;
But the heart and mind still dream,
think big, and routinely feel invincible!

I mourn the fleeting innocence of twelve;
A time before adolescence and hormones took control,
The innocence of infinite possibility,
Keeper of all worthwhile knowledge and experience.

But twelve year olds don't get to travel
On really cool corporate trips
order room service,
drive their own car,
or simply say 'thanks but no thanks'
to a request that just doesn't appeal.

OK, I'm not twelve anymore,
But adulthood has its share of perks as well.

I was afraid as we contemplated starting a family. It wasn't about the worth or sufficiency of a child. It was about stepping into a reality of infinite unknowns and outcomes. It was about questioning my qualifications and ability as a mother. Wouldn't a certain amount of fear and reluctance simply be human?

Mystery of Motherhood

My reluctance for motherhood
Had nothing to do with you.
You were an unknown, a mystery,
I barely knew myself.
Knowledge possessed provided evidence
Of a woman-child ill prepared to nurture.
The little girl inside of me quivered to think
Of our being responsible for another innocent soul.
Wouldn't it be kinder to take a pass?
Let someone else suckle and protect you;
While I remained prisoner of my tightly bound emotions,
Where nothing would be demanded that might crack those bonds?
Yet, I let myself be convinced at the moment of conception;
Pushing the fear aside;
Stepping reluctantly into the adventure of a lifetime.

You remained a mystery, not quite real, yet a part of me.
So you curled and twisted and put off the inevitable,
Waiting for the maternal welcome mat to be unfurled.
Until, at your birth, you and I became a team
Engaged in a fierce battle of life and death,
Breech and butt first you emerged;
A warrior sporting battle scars to prove it.

With wonder and awe at our accomplishment
I looked into your eyes; I held you in my arms,
The mystery was resolved,
Our hearts were eternally tethered.
I acknowledge the miracle.
I fell in love with my son.

I was struck with the poignancy of the death of a friend's daughter with the realization that she died on the same day, in the same hospital where she was born 35 years earlier.

I believe life and death are simply transitions between this world and our real home. The space in between becomes an opportunity for experiencing an infinite array of emotions and wisdom which we take home as souvenirs of our time in Earth School.

Full Circle

An infant's cry heralds the soul's transition
into human form.
I am here, it is my choice!
I am ready to experience both
the joy and pain of flesh and bones.

I have chosen my companions wisely, this I know.
The journey will be long and the lessons sometimes hard;
My choices not always crisp and clear,
But always mine!

Experiences await, choices abound, I live fully,
Embracing adventures and a lifetime of learning,
Until I come full circle at the end of this experience,
Back to a place of transition and I reflect with peace,
Grateful for love forever imprinted
on the surface of my soul.

My goals accomplished, my purpose complete;
The gentle sigh of my soul's transition
Alerts the angels of my return home.

Moments

Moments that soften the heart
And gladden the spirit
Become crystalline memories
To be cherished and shared.

Celebrate the moments!

Ethereal beauty of a mature woman,
Polished to perfection
By the sorrows and celebrations of life.

Eyesight diminished,
Insight strengthened;
The twinkle of youth
Cannot be denied.

A comfort,
A haven,
In her arms
There is love!

I am familiar with this emotional place. The choice is simple; choose to heal the pain and the emotional issues attached to it, or die. Not immediately, of course. Even I'm not that dramatic! But to ignore an opportunity for healing and continue on the lesser path would mean death for my spiritual growth and eventually my physical body.

I have been poised on the verge of just such a choice before. I chose the longer, scarier path to healing. I chose the journey of growth and exploration, and when I find myself standing at one of those crossroads and the easier, shorter path seems almost irresistible, I cling to that six letter word and remind myself there is hope in healing.

Almost

Pebbles of pain ripples through my body
until I am numb with familiarity.
Soon it will take a full grown
rock of discomfort to get my attention.
My body, My barometer;
An early warning system of unhealthy habits and beliefs;
Amazing how much easier to acclimate to pain
than to embrace change.
Today the omnipotent boulder is poised
on the cliff above;
Teetering slightly in my direction.

I find myself at yet another crossroad.
Ever at choice;
I am fearful of the road that winds
into the distant future of unknowns;
Almost willing to accept the crashing oblivion
at the end of this very short path;

Almost . . .

Once I finally get through all the accumulated emotions used to justify my anger and sense of injustice, I find myself in a neutral place we call forgiveness.

It doesn't mean I necessarily want to 'hang out' with that person; and indeed, it sometimes brings confirmation that they no longer belong in my life. Forgiving means I am no longer controlled by the anger and blame I have attached to the situation.

Forgiveness is a freedom which is hard to describe; it is a freedom that must be experienced!

Forgiveness

I forgive you
Not because
You are worthy
Or deserving
Or even because you ask.

I forgive you
Because I am weary
Of the burden,
Of the anger,
Hatred and blame!

I allow the breath
To unlock the chains of blame
Imprisoning my heart,
Only to find it was
Simply a fragile ribbon of silk
Easily dispersed to the wind,
And I soar!

Sometimes I wake in the middle of the night with words or phrases sliding through my mind. I have learned to get up and write these down knowing I will either forget in the morning and mourn the loss of an insight, or I won't get any more sleep because of the endless looping marquee of words.

On this night, when I looked at what I had written before easing back into bed, I grimaced. Bits and pieces were scrawled all over my pad, making no sense at all. A week later I found the pad tucked in my desk and began to see structure here and there; realizing it was not one, but three messages.

This process of writing and revelation never ceases to amaze me, and I'm thankful I can rely on my 'blind faith' to help me honor all experiences, whether or not they make sense at the time.

Resolve

Stubborn perseverance
Blind faith
Desperation
Intention
Chaos and questioning
Dogged forward motion
Seeking the peace of certainty.

Revelation

Vision sharpens
Mist evaporates
Clarity
Focus
Purpose
Pulls me softly into
The brilliance of knowing.

The Other Side of Forgiveness

Blazing betrayal fades.
Ragged emotion is soothed.
Pain dissipates.
As I lay down my gauntlet,
Overwhelmed by its uselessness,
I experience not the concept of peace,
But the reality.
Deep breath;
I am free!

My heart ached for the seemingly kind, gentle woman as I watched her story unfold on TV. It was inconceivable that she had brutally killed her mother with a hammer. In a single moment the wounded and abused child inside her defended against an enemy long ago neutralized but seemingly powerful and overwhelming.

Unhealed nor released, past pain lies dormant . . . a time bomb waiting for the spark to bring it into the present, often with disastrous or inappropriate results.

A Course in Miracles tells us our function here is Forgiveness. Today I take time for an emotional inventory. Is there someone or something I haven't forgiven and released? Today is a good time to start.

Unhealed pain from the past
Intrudes on the present,
Assuming control.

For an instant,
All is lost
In its power.

The person who needs anti-depressants is often the last to realize or accept it. Once the chemical imbalance is rectified, I begin to question whether I really need it after all. It is a paradox but I am drawn to give it a go without the medication.

I feel heavy, burdened without it and feel like ME with it. It's a 'no-brainer' but the human part of the equation is forever questioning . . . do I really need this?

Being Human

I know better!
Research, investigated
Analyzed and categorized,
I am informed!

Educated
Empowered
Enlightened,
And yet, I waffle.

Weakness reinforced,
Deny
Rationalize
Defend and ignore
The tiny pills
Bringing balance
Harmony
Authenticity
The real me.

One more trip to despair,
One more tumble down the rabbit hole,
The contrast of before and after
Always reminding me
Who I really am.

I know better,
But then, I am human.

Diamonds of the Deep

Sunlight reflects off the ever changing surface of the sea;
Fireflies on speed, light bends, dances, disappears;
Reborn on the next crest,
Creating a unique tableau of intensity and sparkle.
Diamonds of the deep; a life span of milliseconds
Not in the least diminished by their brevity.

Past glories
Taunt today's slower pace;
Their mocking laughter
Hollow, challenging.

Over exertion confirms the truth
Of passing time and diminished strength.
Ache and pain are unwelcome reminders
Of neglect and arrogance of the body.

Yesterday's rapid walk on the beach was exhilarating.
Today's slower pace more fitting for reflection.
Deliberate steps move down the beach;
Wet sand cupping each digit in a simple celebration of life.

Someday, when I am incapable of even this leisurely stroll,
I hope babies I once carried to the edge of the sea
Will, in turn, transport me to this place with nostalgia
And I will remember to be grateful, as I am now,
For the experience of the present.

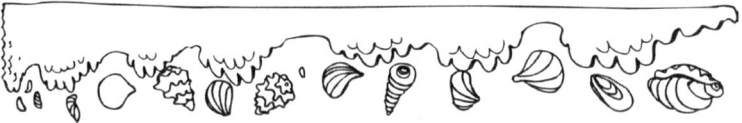

While hiking in Boynton Canyon in Sedona, Arizona, a very clear message was whispered to me on the wind, "Do not take the rocks!"

We had been told to be open to the possibility of messages in this very spiritual place, either personal or for the group. I thought this was surely for the group when I suddenly remembered a small box I had at home containing bits and pieces of previous travels. Small rocks, sea shells, even interesting twigs had somehow made it home with me from many faraway places.

Later, I shared **Captives** with the group and confessed that I had taken rocks from Sedona the last time I was there. Sedona has a very sacred feel and the red rocks are part of that. Removing them without permission is not a good thing, and it was clear to me that the red rocks and soil sitting in a glass jar in my office at home had to be returned.

My husband joined me in Sedona the next day and he agreed to put my 'captive' Sedona rocks in a zip lock bag and bring them to me so I could return them to the place they belong. It may sound weird, I get that, but sometimes you just have to trust Spirit, go with the feeling, and follow where it leads.

Captives

Treasurers gathered on a faraway land,
Left in boxes or bags awaiting the perfect occasion
For remembrance.
Their frustration mixes with mine;
Purpose interrupted,
Not honored.

Do not remove the rocks!
The sign was crystal clear,
Yet I took one anyway,
Feeling the thrill of the dormant rebel.
Had it been a request, not a mandate,
I might have hesitated; or maybe not!

Treasures from my travels,
So urgent and important at the time
Only to be abandoned on my return,
Twigs and seeds become dust
To be scattered on foreign terrain.

In unison they clamor for release,
And I set them free!
The relief of their desperation eases mine
As I remember the joy I tried to capture
By holding a piece of Mother Earth captive.

The violent dream gripped me and I woke shivering. I felt my whole being was in danger of being overrun by evil. After a few deep breaths, I was reminded that it was really up to me if I wanted more love and understanding in the world. What I perceive as evil might be neutralized by the willingness to give up my judgment of others and, more importantly, of myself.

Unconditional Love

Indiscriminate hatred seeps into the soil of the heart,
Choking and destroying souls seduced by its power;
Reeking of the blood and hopelessness
Of innocent lives destroyed,
Poisoning good intention,
Creating fear and its natural, violent response.

Unconditional love, antidote in seemingly short supply,
Rationed to the deserving and worthy . . . What irony!
A commodity that grows only by sharing,
Hoarded and held hostage to fear's reign.

Unbind love, pour it out with abandon
Before we are consumed by this epidemic.

I watched in fascination as the black and yellow spider worked feverishly to complete her task. A long ago phobia of spiders rippled in the back of my mind, urging me to smash the small egg sack and reduce the number of arthropods in my yard.

A mother's compassion was stronger than the old fear, and I could not destroy her precious children. I walked away, glad that I chose love instead of fear.

I will, however, be happy if our paths don't cross again soon!

Survival of the Species

Twisting
Turning
Scraping
Gathering
Cool breeze interlaced with summer's heat
Inflames the biological urge.
Survival of the species wrapped in silk,
Spun tightly; stashed in safety,
Awaiting birth.

Cycle complete, she rests!
She has done all she can for her children.
The next adventure is theirs.

I spent the day clearing weeds and debris from the Koi pond, and noticed the little wild rose has again made an appearance.

It has been over 20 years since my son brought the tiny plant to me from the forest; a sad looking plant hanging out of a plastic grocery bag. It had one small, flat pink flower. I was touched with his thoughtfulness and immediately placed it at the corner of our vegetable garden, wondering if it would survive the transition from forest to suburbia.

Little did I know that it would not only survive but thrive on the nutrient enriched soil. It spread like wildfire, and it didn't take long to realize an occasional trimming was no match for this aggressive plant.

Over the years, trees have matured, shading our garden which has now been converted into the Koi pond. Wild Rose doesn't seem to mind the neighborhood changes. Not even the flagstones deter her. She now peeks tentatively through the pebbles separating the stones and finds her way to the surface.

I sit on the stones today and find that I do not have the desire to continue this battle. She won't bloom where she's planted but she will surely survive and sometimes that's all any of us can do.

Wild Rose

I've trimmed it
Sprayed it
Even dug it up by the roots.
Efforts that slow, but do not eradicate.
Wild Rose returns to stretch her aggressive arms
To the heavens, drinking in sunlight,
Falling back to earth
Seeking purchase on the damp soil.

Planted in an inconvenient place,
She doesn't seem to mind being unwelcome.
Blooms practically non-existent,
Small, sharp thorns abundant
She brings no added value to the area
Except an excellent lesson in persistence.
Today that is enough.
I settle for containment
Instead of extermination.

Look at Me

Look at me; into my eyes.
See my humanity; allow me to see yours.
The miracle of connectivity transforms
This antiseptic, sterile environment
Into a place of safety, comfort, and healing.

Rather than a warehouse for pain,
A jumble of symptoms and diagnoses
Punctuated by plastic chairs and lumpy beds;
Human connection facilitates repair of body and soul.
We share the mutual goal of healing.

Look at me; see who I am
Before I am lost to the hopeless darkness of anonymity.

They are once again taking control,
This menagerie of thoughts and feelings,
An assortment of gut wrenching
Head pounding
Heart stopping
Feelings!
How I hate it when they visit,
These distant relatives I keep at bay
Locked in a closet
Out of sight, out of mind - right?
For a time they rest quietly
I convince myself I have mastered them
They are circus lions;
I am the tamer, with whip and chair.
They perform clever tricks at my simple command.
I am in control.

Over time I become exhausted with the effort,
Teeth are bared - not part of the plan
Sharp
Deadly
Out of control
They bite and gnaw at the bones of my soul
Demanding release from the prison
I have constructed to contain their passion,
The judgements I have issued,
This one good - this one bad, must stay out of sight
Hidden
Shh, no one must know you are part of my family tree
Back in the cage, we can all rest until the next visit.

Gotta Do's

What might I do today
Without these 'gotta do's'?
Endless lists of do's and don't
Fetch and tote,
Errands and reminders!
If only . . .

I might lie abed, drifting
Between sleep and awakening;
Aimlessly wandering the corridors
Of dreams and imagination.

I might
Climb mountains,
Fight battles,
Slay dragons,
Soar on wings of silver.

I might
Dangle a toe in a cool stream,
Watch clouds morph into sky birds,
Write a masterpiece,
Become famous,
Travel the world.

What would I do today
Without these 'gotta do's?

I crawl to the edge of my comfort zone,
Belly flat, head down
Testing my resolve.
I know there is a prize to be claimed
Inside the darkness of the abyss.
Am I brave enough to own it?

I must stand; step beyond this familiar place;
Once again experience the challenge of the unknown.
A deep breath
Inhale
Exhale
Tentatively I touch the darkness
Hesitant
Unsure

Somehow my body has decided for me.
I cross that barrier of my own creation,
To find I have brought the light with me!
There is excitement disguised as fear;
Revealed in the light of a new experience.

The boundaries of comfort have expanded.
The edge is again barely visible far in the distance,
Awaiting another day of exploration.

. . . if the world were perfect, it could not improve and so would lack "true perfection', which depends on progress . . .

Vanini (1585 - 1619)

I am not perfect,
And why would I want to be?
I still have caves to explore,
Lessons to learn,
And new songs to sing.

I will dance naked in the moonlight,
And laugh if I am caught out.
I will shout my truth at the top of my lungs,
Although it may be an unwelcome guest,
And not at all what you expected.

I am past weary of the standards of others.
It is my time and my day,
Which I will use wisely, and a little foolishly;
For one is not exclusive of the other.

To be perfect is to be complete,
Finished, beyond improvement;
So unbelievably boring and uninteresting
That I hug my imperfections and cuddle my flaws,
They are the very things that keep me alive
And moving forward.

Love me or love me not - it does not matter;
For I will love myself enough for us both!

Mourn:
To feel or express sorrow or grief.
To grieve or lament for the dead.

Missed - Not Mourned

I miss your smile.
I miss hearing you say, "I love you".
I miss the feel of your arms around me.
I miss your patience for a schoolgirl's silly excitement.
I miss watching you love my kids and grandkids,
But I no longer mourn your passing.

Lessons learned and love shared
Remain to be cultivated and cherished.
Your loving heart is still,
But your love is a forever gift,
Held close to my heart
Cascading to future generations!

Beginnings and Endings

Each new beginning
Marks the close of a chapter.

Each closed chapter
Becomes a cherished memory,
      richly embellished
      Unique experiences
      a lifetime of friendships.

Sustained by these treasures
Of what came before,
      we step out on faith
      to embrace a future
      filled with promise.

Welcome to the beginning . . .

More Poetry by this author

Journey of a Dream

available on our website

www.JourneyofaDream.com